These Book Belong To :

Welcome
to the Team !

Date :

Date :

Date :

Date :

Date :

Date :

Date :

Date :

Date :

Date :

Date :

Date :

Date :

Date :

Date :

Date :

Date :

Date :

Date :

Date :

Date :

Date :

Date :

Date :

Date :

Date :

Date :

Date :

Date :

Date :

Date :

Date :

Date :

Date :

Date :

Date :

Date :

Date :

Date :

Date :

Date :

Date :

Date :

Date :

Date :

Date :

Date :

Date :

Date :

Date :

Date :

Date :

Date :

Date :

Date :

Date :

Date :

Date :

Date :

Date :

Date :

Date :

Date :

Date :

Date :

Date :

Date :

Date :

Date :

Date :

Date :

Date :

Date :

Date :

Date :

Date :

Date :

Date :

Date :

Date :

Date :

Date :

Date :

Date :

Date :

Date :

Date :

Date :

Date :

Date :

Date :

Date :

Date :

Date :

Date :